D1559004

PORTRAITS OF
DARKNESS

A
Good Friday
Tenebrae
Service

STEPHEN V. DOUGHTY

C.S.S. Publishing Co., Inc.

PORTRAITS OF DARKNESS

9815 / ISBN 1-55673-104-3

PRINTED IN U.S.A.

Preface

Reflections on the Service

Tenebrae and The Passion According to The Gospel of Mark. This service draws on two traditions from the Holy Week observance. The Tenebrae Service dates back to at least the eighth century. Tenebrae means "shadows" in Latin and the Tenebrae Service is a time of commemorating the suffering and death of Jesus. In many churches, candles are extinguished during the service as a sign of the passage from light to darkness.

From at least the early Middle Ages there also springs the Good Friday tradition of meditating on a full passion narrative from any of the four Gospels. In this tradition worshipers would follow closely the events from Jesus' struggle in the garden through his betrayal, judgment, crucifixion, and finally his burial in the tomb. Narrators, or sometimes choruses, would present the events of Scripture and offer meditations on Jesus' passion while the congregation responded with prayers and songs.

Portraits of Darkness is a one-hour service which presents the full passion account in the Gospel of Mark. Readers share the Scripture and offer meditations on eight different portraits Mark paints of the darkness which encompassed Jesus. After each meditation except the last a candle is extinguished and the congregation responds with an appropriate devotional hymn. At the conclusion of the service one candle remains lighted as a sign both of the light which lingered in the minds of Jesus' most faithful followers and as an image of the far greater light which breaks forth on Easter morning. Following the traditions of Tenebrae and Passion services, the worshipers depart from the sanctuary in silence.

Participants: *Portraits of Darkness* is designed for any number of participants. A simple and meaningful arrangement is to have the pastor lead the Invitation to Worship, the Prayer of Preparation, and pronounce the Benediction, and then to have eight laypersons responsible for sharing the "portraits." Each of these persons reads the Scripture, offers the meditation, shares the prayer and then extinguishes a candle. Another arrangement is to have one person responsible for the opening and closing of the service, another for reading the Scripture passages and a third for sharing the meditations and prayers.

Setting and Presentation: The eight candles may be set forth in a variety of ways. Some churches may use a centrally-placed candelabrum and a single candle placed nearby. Others may place the candles on individual stands, grouping seven close together and one slightly separated. It is also possible to construct a cross with holes in it for seven candles. Properly braced, the cross can lean at an angle with the candles arising straight from holes bored in the cross arm and the upright piece. The eighth candle can be placed nearby.

A simple bulletin can indicate the opening portions of the service, the eight portraits with their Scripture passages, and the hymns to be sung. This will save the announcing of hymns and will help maintain focus on the quiet movements of the service itself. The opening and final hymns may be sung standing, with the other hymns sung as the congregation responds from its pews or chairs. For a closing which is appropriate to the mood of the service, an invitation to depart in silence may either be included in the bulletin or shared at the time of the Benediction.

The Service of Tenebrae

PRELUDE

THE INVITATION TO WORSHIP
> Leader: We are invited to witness the great acts of our Savior's love.
>
> **People: We are invited to look within ourselves and examine our lives.**
>
> Leader: We are invited to listen for the words he would speak to us.
>
> **People: We are invited to see deeply into the ways we are to follow.**
>
> Leader: Let us then seek aid for the time that lies ahead.
>
> **People: Amen**

PRAYER OF PREPARATION — *(By the leader or in unison)*
O Gracious and Loving God, by your Spirit create within us now the stillness that we need. May we look steadily upon the pictures you set before us in your word. When we see the shadows that gathered around your Son, may we have the courage to look within ourselves and see where we have helped to cast those shadows. When we catch images of the warmth and brightness of your love, may we know that, in spite of our weakness, this love shines for us all. These things we ask so that this time of reflection may truly be a time of growing closer, deeper in our bonds with you. In the name of your Son, Our Savior, we pray. Amen

HYMN — "Go To Dark Gethsemane"

Temptation

THE SCRIPTURE READING   Mark 14:26-42

THE MEDITATION

Temptation arose early in the darkness and was working quietly within the disciples, as temptation often does. Only for Judas was it anything dramatic, that sudden urge to tell all, to betray boldly, to gather up the cash and flee. For the others it was far subtler. Temptation came softly in the too-easy confidence that they would never betray him, that they would always watch by his side.

Jesus alone knew what was really taking place within each of them. He warned: "Peter, you will betray me." Peter did not believe it. Jesus urged them: "Watch and pray that you may not enter into temptation." They must have looked on him with sleepy eyes. "Of course, Master, we will do just as you say!" they answered and then, not even knowing what they did, rolled over and dozed off again.

It did not matter so much that they were tempted. That had happened to them before. That happens to us all. What mattered was that they gave in. As Jesus put it, they "entered into" the paths of temptation that lay before them.

And it is too easy for us to look on this scene and berate them. It is too easy to say, "Had I been there, I *never* would have slept!" Yet that is just the kind of self-confidence that let the disciples drop their guard, and lets us drop our own.

What we view in this scene is a perfect portrait of how temptation works. We grow confident, sure of ourselves, and beneath that confidence temptation sneaks in. It lays hold as we close our eyes to what is really happening. And when we awake, we find that we are betraying all that we hold most dear.

PRAYER: O Loving Lord, save us from overconfidence. Awaken us to temptation's quiet ways. May we be wise enough to see its strength and mature enough to admit our need for your help. Help us to watch and pray that we may not abandon you and the paths you have called us to. Amen

(Extinguish the first candle.)

HYMN — "'Tis Midnight; And On Olive's Brow"

One Ran Away

THE SCRIPTURE READING   Mark 14:43-52

THE MEDITATION

The image suddenly is of a mob. They mutter, carry clubs, brandish swords as they press into the garden. At their head Judas gives his kiss and utters the betraying word, "Master!" Then, after the briefest moment, the image shifts and is of another mob, not the one with swords and clubs. It is the mob of disciples scattering, cloaked in the darkness of robes drawn tight across their faces, fleeing into the night. Like water spilt upon the ground they shoot out in all directions and are instantly gone.

And just as suddenly as all of this the image becomes no longer of a mob, but of only one. "A young man followed him" we are told. Was he more daring than the others? Perhaps. Was he anxious to know what would happen next? Did he wish to see it for himself? Perhaps these things too.

In an instant strong hands gripped him by the shoulders. "We caught another," cried a voice. The young man struggled, lurched, pulled against those hands, and then broke free. He fled into the darkness terrified . . . terrified and naked. His only garment hung limp in the hands of his would-be captor.

One ran away. And in his terror and his nakedness he is the image of all the others who fled. He is the image of any who have ever denied the Lord. He is the perfect picture of us when in our timidity, or our fear of what others might think, we deny Jesus by drawing back from his ways. We then are uncovered, shown for what we are in our weakness and in our desperate need of the one who goes to the Cross alone.

PRAYER: O Lord, forgive us for those times when we have

8

wanted to stay close to you and then suddenly drawn back, turned aside, raced, exposed and weak, into other paths. Renew within us, Lord, the will to follow you wherever you go. Amen

(Extinguish the second candle.)

HYMN — "Beneath The Cross of Jesus"

False Witnesses

THE SCRIPTURE READING   Mark 14:53-65

THE MEDITATION
    From childhood they had learned the ancient command, "You shall not bear false witness." Now, in the pressure of the moment, they could barely tell lies fast enough. "He said he would destroy the temple and in three days raise another!" "He speaks blasphemy against the Lord our God!"
    The same thing happened with these lies that always happens with lies. They spread more darkness over those who told them than over the person they lied against. Jesus, in effect, acknowledged, "I am the Son of God." Nothing they said could change that. He remained the same. Those who told the lies, however, now had to stand within the darkness of their own distorted vision. The false witness they bore hung like a cloud between them and the Master. They saw not "Lord," not "Savior," not "Son of God." They could only see the words they spoke. Traitor. Fanatic. Blasphemer against the living God.
    In our own age it is possible to bear false witness against Jesus in quieter ways, but the result is the same. It is possible to see him as simply a very good man, the best that ever lived. Such a vision, however, can blind us to the reality of divine power breaking forth in our world. It is possible to see him the one who did indeed shatter the bonds of death,

but if the hope of the resurrection is all we look to, then we shall surely miss what he calls us to do right now for the victims of poverty, injustice, and war.

What we most need to do is what those first persons in Jesus' presence needed to do. Be silent. Let him bear witness to himself. Let him impress himself upon our lives.

PRAYER: Clear our minds of distorted images of you. Save us from bearing false witness, even unintentionally. Lord Jesus, let us see you as you really are. Amen

(Extinguish the third candle.)

HYMN — "There Is A Green Hill Far Away"

Tears

THE SCRIPTURE READING   Mark 14:66-72

THE MEDITATION

It would be almost impossible to paint what Peter was like just after the cock crowed for the second time. A good artist could catch the surface details — the bowed form, the head turned sharply to one side, a hand drawn roughly across the face to catch fast-falling tears. A great artist might hint at depths of anguish which lay behind the tears. But could anyone portray what even Peter in those moments did not grasp? Could any show that those tears brought with them at least the chance of a fresh start?

Peter wept bitterly, but his tears of remorse lay far closer to the truth about himself than those words he spoke with such assurance, "If I must die with you, I will not deny you." Tears now burned away the dull clouds of illusion. Tears washed out the darkness of a mistaken trust in himself. For the moment all he could see was a terrible emptiness. Could it be, though, that because of those tears he would one day view himself and his Lord more clearly than he ever had before?

Remorse is always bitter. We lash out with words of anger, then ache with regret. We speak with impatience, then wish with all our heart we had shown kindness instead. We betray a trust, then weep inwardly when we come to our senses. Yet for all the pain, remorse can open us for healing. Tears of regret, like Peter's tears, can clear our sight.

PRAYER: Lord, teach us not to hide our regrets from ourselves. We surely cannot hide them from you. And when we have wronged another, when we have in some way denied you, may we listen to the hurt we feel inside . . . and may we learn. Amen

(Extinguish the fourth candle.)

HYMN — "When I Survey the Wondrous Cross"

A Crowd Stirred Up

THE SCRIPTURE READING   Mark 15:1-15

THE MEDITATION

Follow for a moment the eyes and ears of the crowd in those last hours before they finally yelled "Crucify!" For days at least some of them had focused on Jesus. They had watched him. They had listened to him. They had begun to draw new life from him. Now all that shifted. Eyes looked no longer on Jesus but on impressive public figures in their flowing robes. Ears no longer listened for his teachings. They listened to what these popular persons had to say. Before the crowd ever betrayed Jesus with its lips it had already betrayed him with its ears and eyes. It looked no longer to him, but to others, for its guidance.

How often darkness spreads this way. Individuals, crowds, whole nations take destructive paths not just because of some undefined weakness. They do so because they look in the wrong direction for guidance. Racism . . .

rampant materialism . . . an arms race that moves ahead full throttle while millions of innocents do not have enough to eat. These are the fruits of a value system that has abandoned, or never found, the proper focus.

We can criticize the crowd for being fickle. It would be far better, though, to try with all diligence to learn from its mistake. There is only one who can truly serve as the source of our values and our deeds. We need to keep our very selves turned to him. Let him and him alone be the source of all that we do.

PRAYER: O Gracious, Loving Lord, you who are the source of all goodness, may we look steadily to you. In public matters, and in our most private deeds, may we have the wisdom to seek your will. And when we have discerned that will, may we possess the courage to do it, even when many others move in a different direction. Amen

(Extinguish the fifth candle.)

ANTHEM (or HYMN) — "My Faith Looks Up To Thee"
verses 1, 2, 3

Struck . . . Mocked . . . Crucified

THE SCRIPTURE READING   Mark 15:16-32

THE MEDITATION

The darkness now deepened in what they did. They struck, mocked, plaited the crown of thorns and pressed it into his skull. They spat on the face that had glowed with compassion. They nailed hands which brought sight to the blind. They crucified the still-young form which had long bent every ounce of strength to share good news with the lost and the lonely. And when at last Jesus hung dying, those not yet satisfied stood and reviled with quick, sharp phrases.

12

They wanted to wring every ounce of twisted pleasure from the moment.

We can stare in horror at the scene. We can fix our minds on brutal acts and battered flesh. This brings home the awesome reality of what they did.

More important, though, we need to look on this scene and consider what Jesus was willing to endure for the sake of divine love. The beating and the mocking and the nailing to an instrument of death are all signs of a terrible human cruelty. It was utterly wrong. Human cruelty in any form is utterly wrong. Yet deeper than the mystery of this darkness is the mystery of a love so great that it would accept even the worst that we can do and accept it in the hope, the battered hope, that we might find the way to life.

PRAYER: Gracious Lord, may we not hide ourselves from what took place. May we keep before us the image of all that you endured. And in that image may we even now see reflected the fulness of your love. Amen

(Extinguish the sixth candle.)

HYMN — "Were You There When They Crucified My Lord" *(Singing two verses — "Were you there when they crucified my Lord?" and "Were you there when they nailed him to the tree?")*

Darkness Over The Land

THE SCRIPTURE READING   Mark 15:33-38

THE MEDITATION
The darkness now grew nearly all-encompassing. It was no longer confined to the hearts of a few who stumbled into temptation. It did not just cloak a single figure who fled terrified into the night, nor did the darkness simply cloud the vision of an unruly mob that bore false witness. The darkness

broke loose. Mark tells us "there was darkness over the whole land."

Consider the darkness. Where did it lie? It lay across fields and homes. It lay across the young, the middle-aged, the old. It spread its shadows over a palace and through the temple of God. Wherever lives had danced and found joy, wherever hope had sprung up with promises of goodness yet to come, the darkness settled. It shut out all visions of a future.

Consider the darkness. Where did it come from? It came from indifference, apathy, jealousy in the human heart. It arose from lives grown insensitive to the good. It grew from lack of trust in the ways of God, lack of courage, lack of will to remain steadfast through a difficult time.

Consider again the darkness. What did it mean? It meant, quite simply, that all hope was gone, extinguished. The best the world had ever seen now died upon the Cross.

The darkness also meant . . . though of this there was only the barest hint . . . the darkness meant that if somehow this darkness should be broken, if somehow this Jesus could overcome the darkness, then hope would shine for all. It would mean that not even the deepest human darkness, not even death itself, could withstand his light. For the moment, though, this possibility lay on no one's mind. He hung on the Cross, and darkness spread over the whole land.

PRAYER: Loving and obedient Lord, grant us courage to look on the darkness which surrounded you at the end. We know that only when we comprehend the depths of those final shadows shall we grow prepared to see the stunning brightness of the victory you died to win. Amen

(Extinguish the seventh candle.)

HYMN — "Were You There When They Crucified My Lord?" *(Singing one verse: "Were you there when they laid him in the tomb?")*

Lingering Light

THE SCRIPTURE READING   Mark 15:39-47

THE MEDITATION

And after Jesus died, a single light seemed to linger. It lingered only in the minds of those who saw most deeply. It hovered there as memory, a wisp of goodness now thought to be utterly gone but which could at least be kept in the mind and recalled from time to time.

Light lingered for the centurion who said, "Truly this man was the Son of God!" He used the past tense when he spoke . . . "*was* the Son of God." To the centurion, like everybody else, it seemed to be completely over. Yet at least there had been, however briefly, a Son of God. The memory of a light, the recollection of a brightness continued in his mind.

Light lingered for the women who stood at a distance and watched it all. It persisted for Joseph of Arimathea who took courage and laid the body in a tomb. It settled on the two Marys who, just before the sabbath began, went to see where the body was laid away. For them all the light endured as but a single spot of brightness. It survived as a thought, deeply felt, that on the Cross they had seen one brighter than the world had ever known.

In time that lingering light would shine more brightly, and with greater life, than they had ever dreamed. But for now, let our thoughts be one with theirs. Let us look deeply enough to know that a light has shown from the Cross and that even the greatest darkness cannot take it from our minds.

PRAYER: O Loving and ever-faithful Lord, may we keep before us the light we have seen on the Cross. In our own times of darkness, and in our seasons of rest and joy, may we look to you. And may we know that the light which continues even now is but a glimmering sign of the brightness that shall be. Amen

(The eighth candle shall remain lighted.)

HYMN — "In The Cross Of Christ I Glory"

BENEDICTION: *(The persons pronouncing the benediction may hold forth the one remaining lighted candle as the following words are spoken.)*
And now may you go forth knowing that the light you have seen shall never depart from you. Even in the places of deepest shadow, nothing shall put it out. May you seek, always, to walk in the warmth and goodness of that light. And may the grace of the Lord Jesus Christ, the love of God, and the Fellowship of the Holy Spirit rest upon you and be with you all, now and forever. Amen

About the Author

From the time of his ordination in 1968, Stephen V. Doughty has served actively in the parish ministry, pastoring first the Presbyterian churches of Chipman and Waddington, New York, and then the Presbyterian Church of Lead, in the Black Hills of South Dakota. Since 1983 he has been pastor and staff director for the six churches of the Northwest Area Ministry, a western Pennsylvania mission of Kiskiminetas Presbytery and the Penn West Conference of the United Church of Christ.

In addition to pastoring and writing, Reverend Doughty is a frequent workshop leader and has taught on the faculty of the Appalachian Regional School for Church Leaders, sponsored by the Commission on Religion in Appalachia. A major focus in his teaching and writing is the intimate relationship between spiritual formation and active ministry on both the personal and social levels.

His hobbies include astronomy, hiking, playing the dulcimer, and learning the lore of the various regions in which he and his family have lived. He has a strong commitment to the life of smaller congregations and serves on his denomination's national planning group for the nurture and support of small churches.

Reverend Doughty is married to Jean McLeod, herself a writer and teacher. They have two teenage children, Kevin and Jan. The four of them have a dog, Albert, who over the past ten years has become a family treasure and, they will tell anyone, is still eager to learn new tricks.